Catholics
Mean Business

Catholics
Mean Business

30 Days to Managing Your Work Week, God's Way

John C. Connell

Outskirts Press, Inc.
Denver, Colorado

Catholics Mean Business
30 Days to Managing Your Work Week, God's Way
All Rights Reserved.
Copyright © 2009 John C. Connell
v3.0

The scripture passages contained here are from The New American Bible, St. Joseph Medium Size Edition, by Catholic Book Publishing Co., New York, N.Y., Copyright 1987, 1980, 1970.

Outskirts Press, Inc.
http://www.outskirtspress.com

ISBN: 978-1-4327-2974-5

Outskirts Press and the "OP" logo are trademarks belonging to Outskirts Press, Inc.

PRINTED IN THE UNITED STATES OF AMERICA

**To my Grandparents,
Clifford & Irene Hansen.**

Table of Contents

Acknowledgements

This would not be possible without the generosity and kindness of the following people: God for the words, my beautiful wife, Lori, for her support & patience, our kids for keeping me focused & for their original custom cover artwork, my proof-reading team – Mom & Dad, Tim Short, Joe Evinsky, my best man Ed Toth, and both Mike (Mr. President) & Maura Sweet.

To my cousin, Fr. James Stenger of St. Peter the Apostle parish in Brookpark, Ohio & my pastor Fr. Paul Lockey of St. Elizabeth Ann Seton parish in Houston, Texas for their valuable theological counsel.

Special thanks to my Editor, Laurie Evinsky, for her sharp eye, faith & friendship & to all the good folks at Outskirts Press.

Introduction

**"How can this book help me
mind my business?"**

Your business. Think about your current job, your most recent paycheck. Is it really yours? You work hard enough for it. You pay the taxes. You incur the costs. You shoulder the responsibility.

But is it really yours?

It is written in the Bible that everything belongs to God, and that the whole world is under Jesus' authority. As a Catholic, do you agree?

Some people, including some Catholics, disregard parts of scripture because they feel it does not apply to them. Others don't bother reading the Bible – on their own time – because they do not know where to begin. Then there are those who want the good news, the wisdom and power available to those who study scripture yet...just don't seem to ever get around to it. They are too busy with the race. There are too many things to be captured, first.

The problem is that they run right past the path to peace, fulfillment, accomplishment, self worth, and yes, even success in business – because in their race they miss the turn at the road named Contribution! You obtain all these things through giving, not receiving.

Think about Rick Warren's mega-million bestseller, "The Purpose Driven Life". That masterpiece starts with one of the best sentences I have ever read: "It's not about you." I came across his book one morning in a Perpetual Adoration chapel. The first page provided validation for my entire approach to life and business.

I have been in sales and territory management for over 15 years. I love the profession. I have enjoyed good years and I have endured bad years. I know the views from the top and bottom.

During my career I have seen many sales people, managers, company owners and other professionals claiming to be Catholic or Christian, leave their faith behind in Church each Sunday. During their work week, they proceed to do whatever they deem necessary to conduct their business, regardless of eternal consequences, or effects on others.

How do you deal with people like this? How do you succeed when it seems like you are the only one playing by the rules? Read on, I know of a ready and powerful antidote.

You may not realize it today, but the Bible is the best business book ever written. If you take this material to heart, it will not fail you. I know because over the past 15 years I have practiced this approach myself. This material can change the course of your career, your life, and your afterlife. The purpose and function of this work is to point you in the direction of greatness.

This is about you and God, your business and your career. I am passionate about this material because *it works*. It can transform your thinking, your job performance and your organization if put into <u>practice</u>.

Do you want to be THE go-to person? Do you want to be the person others come to for advice? Do you want to consistently meet deadlines, goals and quotas with less stress? Yes, I said less stress. Do you want to be able to recall what is needed to settle yourself down when the deadlines are looming, and help yourself breathe easier and sleep like a baby?

Do you want to recession-proof your career? Do you want to be an island of calm when everyone else sees the market turn and fears the worst? Do you want your business or career to outgrow its current problems?

God does. But His plan for you requires your participation. It's time to go to work.

This book addresses the four main relationships we all wrestle with as we write the sagas of our careers: You and God, You and Others, You and Money & You and Work. Chapters are broken up into "Days". Over the next thirty days, take a couple moments – each morning – to read a short and specific chapter pertaining to one of the four relationships. Then think about what you read on your way to work and keep an open mind as to where those thoughts may lead you. That's it. That's your task. God will do the rest, if you let Him.

Sound easy? It is. God's burden is always light.

DAY 1
You & God

"For I know well the plans I have in mind for you, says the Lord, plans for your welfare, not your woe! Plans to give you a future full of hope." Jeremiah 29:11

The first time I read this verse I was several hours into a job interview that would change my life. I flew from Ohio to Texas to meet with a group of gentlemen from a large company. The interview took all day and moved me in and out of several different offices and even through a couple of restaurants.

At one point, I sat across from the manager who wanted to hire me. I looked over and saw the quote hanging on a cubicle wall. I chose to take it as a sign – a confirmation – and said yes to his offer. Saying yes, however, meant packing up my family and moving across country, away from the only comfort zone I ever knew.

And you know what? Every detail of the relocation fell right into place. Our tiny "starter" home sold in just two weeks, in the middle of winter! The transplant of our lives was not without challenge, but in hindsight, flowed with God's choreography.

We all have our own plans. However, none of those plans will ever be as "meaningful" as God's plans are for us. **We are made on purpose – our place in time is no accident.**

Time has often reminded me that believing in this scripture verse was not just sound business advice, but a huge blessing to me and my family. The blessing was not just the career move, but the relocation as well. And the man who hired me became a great mentor to me and a true friend.

So how do we know what the plan is for us? How do we figure out if our plans are THE plans? That is our common challenge. That is where our common faith, as Catholic Professionals, comes in.

In my life and career, the only tool I found to decode the mystery is prayer. ***ASK Him.*** God will let us know the answers in His time. And if we remain open-minded, He will alert us when the time comes. Who knows, He may even post a sign on the wall.

DAY 2
You & Work

**"You see a man skilled in his work?
He shall stand in the presence of kings;
he will not stand in the presence of
obscure men." Proverbs 22:29**

It is said that repetition is the mother of skill. Do you practice your business? Do you want to get better or just be paid better? Are you hungry for growth or just in a comfortable rut?

This was the first verse I read in a gift book I received as a graduation present from my Godmother. The little book was made of card stock and listed Scripture quotes that directly pertained to business. I read it countless times and kept it on my desk for years. It was a catalyst to my business approach, a fire starter.

Other translations of this verse substitute the

word "diligent" for "skilled" and the phrase "substantial men" for the word "kings."

Substantial men, kings, rulers, decision makers. You want to influence them? Do you want to travel in their circles and have them seek your counsel?

Practice. Hone your skills. Be diligent. Find one thing you can do – today – to become better at your job.

Manage your career, not just your year. Look beyond your present station. Love persistence. Never quit. This verse is not just a proverb, it is a prediction. It is a success guarantee.

DAY 3
You & Money

"What profit is there for one to gain the whole world yet lose or forfeit himself?"
Luke 9:25

We do not live on this earth forever. Money is only a means to an end. You are here for a reason — and it is not just to grab a bunch of cash.

This life is temporary; the next is permanent. Let that "truth" sink into your bones. How will it impact your decision making today? If you made a habit of reminding yourself of that fact, how would you treat others, handle interruptions, conduct yourself in meetings and answer requests?

And because actions always speak louder than words, *how would your actions answer the Lord's question in today's verse?*

DAY 4
You & Others

**"The just man's lips nourish many,
but fools die for want of sense."
Proverbs 10:21**

Who do you go to for guidance when you really need direction? Think about what that person possesses to earn your confidence. Chances are they seem well-rooted and centered, a person without ego. They will have more experience and may have more money than you, at the moment, however their real riches will be in what eludes you.

A certain level of financial success does not ensure people will seek you out. And a prestigious position on the corporate ladder, a fancy job title, does not reveal anything about a person's ability to teach, counsel and guide.

Wisdom does not require power and fortune

when choosing a residence for itself. However, having wisdom can lead to those conditions. The clear path that wisdom provides is what we all need to keep from floundering. With it we become a homing beacon in the dark for others.

Wisdom, far more than money or status, makes us valuable to those around us. Take your first steps in that direction. **Open your Bible to any one of the Gospels and read a passage before work.**

DAY 5
You & Money

"No one can serve two masters. He will either hate one and love the other, or be devoted to one and despise the other. You cannot serve God and mammon.*"
Mark 6:24

Hate money to love God? It begs the question: why does it have to be one or the other? As hard working providers for our families, we should not feel forced to lead a "double-life". Commerce is as much a part of our existence as the planet itself, so money dealings remain unavoidable.

But the key words here are "serve" and "masters". Whose way, yours or God's, will you subscribe to as you plow through the work week? This verse is all about intent.

Intent does not have anything to do with

amounts, whether you have a lot or a little. Your current balance is just that, current. You can serve a master with any amount. So be honest with yourself. Intent is the heart of the matter. And inside the heart is a place only you and God share.

Today, look to give a little money away without any concern for repayment.

*Mammon: Riches, material wealth or the personification of money as a deity.

DAY 6
You & Work

**"Can any of you by worrying add a
single moment to your life-span?"
Matthew 6:27**

How many hours, days, weeks or months of our lives
have we spent worrying about things we can never
control? Often times, the corporate world doesn't
seem happy unless we are stressed out. I shudder
to think what my worrying has kept me from.

It is amazing how only Christ can speak to us, in
such an awakening way, with so few words. Worry
only robs us of our vitality. If we let it, worry will
paralyze us and keep us from our missions in life.

And why do we worry? We worry because there
are plenty of things beyond our control. Contrary to
almost every self-help book on the market, I would
like to point out that **we are not the center of**

the universe! We are only here for a short time and we must keep busy, living our purpose. ***Spend your time only on what matters: God and others – your relationships – both corporate and personal.***

If you disagree, consider this. In the fall of 2008, my family and our south Texas neighborhood were still recovering from Hurricane Ike, which chewed up Galveston and parts of Houston in late summer. We were all busy fixing fences and repairing rooftops. The constant thump of distant hammers could be heard throughout the area. The situation was even worse for those along the Gulf Coast.

We are all just a natural disaster away from being homeless. No amount of worry could have altered the course of that hurricane. Most of us are only a merger or a corporate belt-tightening away from being on the outside looking in. When stuff disappears, what we are left with is what's most important - each other. Why spend time and energy on anything else?

DAY 7
You & God

"Ask and it will be given to you; seek and you will find; knock and the door will be opened." Matthew 7:7

I used to waste time over-preparing for difficult meetings. I would try to anticipate and practice my responses to potential hard questions and objections. I fancied myself clever for thinking ahead, like in chess. Did it ever help? No. In hindsight, I was too focused on the differences between my "opponents" and myself.

I stopped wasting my time and energy when I realized I was not attending those meetings by myself. If God was everywhere and knew all things, then He could join me in my appointments and on all my sales calls. I just had to invite Him.

These days, meetings are easy and sales calls

are nothing but fun, even when I don't make the sale. I spend my time looking for connections and let God handle the difficulties.

I do my part and God does His. ***I recommend praying today with <u>expectation</u> in God's partnership and providence.*** In return, He will open new doors and show you what you are looking for. He will be glad to emcee your entire day.

DAY 8
You & Money

"With me are riches and honor, enduring wealth and prosperity." Proverbs 8:18

If a friend and confidant approached you with a secret - the tried-and-true means of acquiring life-long success - I bet you would give him your undivided attention.

The "me" in this verse refers to Wisdom. Wisdom is not only the key to obtaining wealth, but keeping it.

Notice that riches are paired with honor here. It is not enough to just have a lot of money. The world has seen a lot of rich, dishonorable people. Only riches with honor and respect are worthy of your labor.

The friend sharing the secret, as you can guess,

is the Lord. He knows what you are capable of and He has BIG plans for those who listen.

Have you handled money in a way that would make the Lord, your parents, mentors, spouse and kids proud?

DAY 9
You & Money

"It is the Lord's blessing that brings wealth, and no effort can substitute for it." Proverbs 10:22

We profess this Proverb every time we pray the Lord's Prayer.

"...Thy will be done.......Give us today our daily bread..." Still, this verse begs a couple questions. If I struggle financially, am I not blessed? Why work so hard if God is going to decide who ends up with the money?

First off, it is through our struggles that two beautiful things happen: we get better and we grow closer to God. I have never been poor, but I have been plenty broke. During those times I have turned to prayer for guidance, grounding and focus. I have always found all three. I also realized how blessed I truly was in other areas of my life and career.

Regarding the second question, we all like to be in control. We like to stand up and take credit for our good fortune. We do not like to think of ourselves as powerless. The good news is that we are not – we always have a role to play.

It is not the amount of money that matters most; it is the actions we take with our incomes that impact our financial blessings. Regardless of corporate or personal revenues, our responsibilities do not change.

Everyone wants wealth NOW, but are you ready for it? Also, consider the fact that as human beings, our definition of wealth may differ from God's. Wealth means more than money. Blessings are not just our talents and treasure. He gives freely to all. His blessings also include His word and His way. ***Use all the above to achieve the <u>enduring</u> wealth of life you seek.***

DAY 10
You & Others

"Do to others whatever you would have them do to you. This is the law and the prophets." Matthew 7:12

The Golden Rule. We can all repeat it to others, but how much conscious effort do we spend trying to apply it on the job? Imagine how our companies, industries and culture would benefit from a more intense application of this directive.

Think about how you want to be treated in the office or on the job site:

- You want to feel appreciated.
- You want to be listened to.
- You want your calls returned.
- You want to be given time to respond to e-mails and other inquiries.

- You want the sovereignty of your personal space maintained.
- You want to be asked, not told, when addressed by your peers.
- You want to feel a part of something important.
- You want camaraderie.
- You want to always be treated with dignity and respect.

On your way into work, think about your co-workers, bosses, customers and suppliers. Regardless of your position at your company, you can lead by example. ***As a Catholic professional, what can you do today, to keep someone else from still wanting these things tonight?***

DAY 11
You & Work

**"Jesus said to them, 'Come after me
and I will make you fishers of men.'"
Mark 1:17**

The Lord went to James and John's place of business, and called them both to something more. That same Lord is calling you too, right where you are.

Even though the story goes on to tell us the first apostles left their work that day to follow Jesus, at other times in the Gospels the disciples are fishing. This tells us they did not permanently abandon their profession.

However, they did take on more responsibility. They volunteered for other duties as an answer to the Lord's call. That calling was for them to look beyond themselves, to see bigger issues and to recognize the significance of their actions and the importance of others.

That same call can be heard today, if we choose to stop and listen. We do not have to quit our jobs and enter the seminary. On the contrary, God wants us to remain at our posts, to illuminate our corporations with our actions, to cast a net within our area of influence and continue the fishermen's vital work.

How can you influence others at work? Are you capitalizing on those opportunities?

DAY 12
You & Others

**"Whatever place does not welcome
you or listen to you, leave there
and shake the dust off your feet in
testimony against them." Mark 6:11**

As a career sales person, I love this verse. It is just wonderful advice from the Lord. Jesus did not command his disciples to curse those who didn't accept their message; He knew rejection would occur. He also knew that no amount of rejection would change the apostles' mission and the goal He had in mind for them. Therefore, he was succinct in instructing the missionaries to ignore the objections, stay focused, and keep moving.

Throughout our careers, we must at times speak our minds, present our cases and persuade others to join us in our endeavors. Objections and rejection are part of the process. Expect it, plan for it, but above all, do not take offense when you experience it.

Keep your eyes on the prize. Stay true to your vision. Keep moving forward. Remember you are where you are on purpose. Your place in time is no accident. ***Take a few minutes today, getting comfortable with the fact that you are part of God's plan for humanity.***

DAY 13
You & Others

**"The memory of the just will be blessed,
but the name of the wicked will rot."
Proverbs 10:7**

Many people labor in vain to create some sort of
personal legacy within their communities and even
society as a whole. In reality, we have no control of
other people's perceptions, experiences or memories once we are gone from this life.

That said there is indeed a way to leave behind
a positive, lasting footprint on others during your
short time here. In business terms, it must be a re-
tail effort, not wholesale.

Make a personal contribution to those within
reach. When is the last time you took a moment to
help someone without being asked? We see people in the corporate world hoard their experiences,

in some trivial, territorial attempt to outshine their peers. Why? At the rate companies merge, restructure or relocate, there is no guarantee you will be working with the same crowd a few years from today. You have an opportunity NOW.

Invest in someone else's future. Lend a hand without being asked. Help someone else taste success. ***Do it today.*** You'll be surprised how good you will feel.

DAY 14
You & God

This is the day the Lord has made; let us rejoice and be glad in it." Psalm 118: 24

Last night you went to sleep fatigued from life and all its current struggles. Well I have good news.

Today is a brand new day. Yesterday is gone forever; it will only live on in memories. Tomorrow is up to God. We cannot control it, we can only prepare for it.

But TODAY is what we have. Today is a gift – even if we have something unpleasant to do. God saw fit to include you in today. You are a part of God's plan; you are a part of His gift.

Once again, we are given a chance to live, love and laugh – even as we work. **Look today to show someone some love. Find something to laugh about. Point out something good about life to someone else. They may really need it.**

DAY 15
You & Work

"A good name is more desirable than great riches, and high esteem, than gold and silver." Proverbs 22:1

How do we recession-proof our careers? How do we bulletproof ourselves at our companies and within our chosen industry? Reeling in revenue and/or eliminating expenses is what the boss or banker would say, but I have seen some do that and still be downsized, right-sized or just plain cut loose anyway, with the stroke of a pen.

I have also seen people reach the top of the corporate ladder, by climbing on and over those around them. They make more money than they could spend, but when they vacate their post, cheers and jeers can be heard from co-workers as their cars leave the parking lot.

Positive cash flow and net profits are how we keep the lights on and the doors open. Becoming skilled at producing these results is integral to success in the corporate world. But that is just being average.

Beyond that, we need to separate ourselves. The fastest way, and the path with the least amount of traffic, is to cultivate the heart of a servant. The givers of this world are treated in kind.

The giver is the kind of person that *smart* companies fight to keep around. Real givers do not discriminate, only serving those that can repay. The servant I am describing lifts everyone up around them. The more people you touch, the more invaluable you become.

How can you be that person at your job – starting today?

DAY 16
You & God

"Have no anxiety at all, but in everything, by prayer and petition, with thanksgiving, make your requests known to God." Philippians 4:6

God knows everything that is going on inside you. Your thoughts, your intents, your fears, your vision, He sees it all. Even better, He knows what you need and He knows how to deliver it to you – or deliver you to *it*.

The only thing He needs is your permission. For reasons that are His alone, He wants to be asked first.

The very next verse in Philippians tells of what happens when you make your requests known to God. It states that God's peace, which "surpasses all understanding", will guard you inside. That is music to our ears, and souls, when we are tossing and turning at night. That is why, as Catholic Professionals, we need to continue to ask Him for help.

He thinks in ways we cannot think. He sees things we cannot see. He understands things we do not understand. He is aware of what escapes us.

Knowledge is power, and He has all the knowledge all the time. He wants to use His power to light your way, and see you safely through every situation. **On the way to work today, talk to Him about what's bothering you.** He has answers, solutions and blessings waiting in reserve.

DAY 17
You & Money

**"Wealth quickly gotten dwindles away,
but amassed little by little, it grows."
Proverbs 13:11**

Pace yourself. The get-rich-quick schemes don't work! Manage your career, not just your year.

Yes, the market can be volatile, but that volatility will only hurt the short-term thinker. Look at the historical average of the stock market, and you will see an impressive track record of growth. Sure there are a few down years amongst those decades (2008 is still fresh in everyone's mind), but with faith and a focus on long-term growth, there will be no financial storms we cannot weather.

That same focus on the future, instead of on just right now, will keep us calm, cool and collected throughout our careers. Always use your long-term priorities as your compass when managing the checkbook.

Where do you see yourself in ten years? Have today's storms subsided by then? **Are you accepting God's guidance today to take you down the right path towards your vision?**

DAY 18
You & Work

"Go to the ant, O sluggard, study her ways and learn wisdom; for though she has no chief, no commander or ruler, she procures her food in the summer, stores up her provisions in the harvest."
Proverbs 6:6-8

This quote reminds me of a sign I once saw in front of a high school. It was early summer and the marquee stood as a final lecture for the recent class of graduates. "Success Operates on a Self-Serve Basis."

We are all capable of bringing to fruition our God-given and grandest dreams. However, the possible realities we envision will be largely determined by our actions and work ethic when not directed by an authority figure.

What do you tend to do when no one else is around? Do you goof-off or press on? The choice is yours, and so is the quality of your future.

DAY 19
You & Money

"But God said to him, 'You fool, this night your life will be demanded of you; and the things you have prepared, to whom will they belong?'" Luke 12:20-21

Our time here is shorter than any of us would like. As we work and save and plan for our futures, at what point are we just building bigger barns? The answer will be different for each of us, due to our situations. But just like back on Day Five, we need to examine our intent.

What are we using our prosperity for? More toys, more house? How does any of that really help us or others?

Yes, we all need to save for a rainy day. That is sound, time tested advice. But we also need to share, to be prepared to give to others, when the rain falls.

He or she who dies with the most toys wins nothing. **Give freely of your time, talent and treasure.**

When we imagine meeting God face to face, we can think of all kinds of things we would like to hear Him say. "You fool," would not top anyone's list.

DAY 20
You & Work

"Better a lowly man who supports himself than one of assumed importance who lacks bread." Proverbs 12:9

Do not tell people your title or job description unless asked. Rather, show people what you do.

These days our corporate world is filled with *Executives of this* or *Vice Presidents of that*. Titles ring hollow – unless infused with meaning by your actions. Words on a business card are invisible to a customer you could not satisfy or a co-worker that struggles without assistance.

If you have a fancy title, what can you do for someone else today, to prove you've earned it? If you do not have a fancy title, what can you do for someone else today, to earn one?

DAY 21
You & God

"You shall not steal." Exodus 20:15

The Catechism of the Catholic Church dedicates almost fourteen pages to this one sentence. This is the collective wisdom of the Church fathers, scholars and saints from over two thousand years. It is nothing short of fascinating!

In only a couple paragraphs, I cannot begin to do the Catechism justice. However, I can offer a couple observations and a little food for today's thought.

It was no accident for this commandment to be the seventh. Seven is a perfect number, and a number attributed to perfection in scripture. God is perfect. God is a giver. We are instructed to follow suit, but the world encourages the exact opposite.

Theft is not just usurping someone else's property. As Catholic professionals, we also have the responsibility of eliminating and avoiding unfair pricing practices, poor work quality, tax evasion, unpaid debts, deceit and unfulfilled commitments and contracts of all types.

In what ways are you temped to steal in your business? As one of God's stewards, what can you do to ensure justice is put into practice?

DAY 22
You & God

"The bread of deceit is sweet to a man, but afterward his mouth will be filled with gravel." Proverbs 20:17

Ever wonder how you can get ahead when it seems like you are the only one playing by the rules? It really stings when the cheaters are self-proclaimed Catholics, Christians or all around "good guys".

Like many of you, I have been lied to and abused on the job and in the course of business. Some of these crosses have been heavy for my family to carry. It is at times tempting to fight fire with fire, and resort to behavior that many would justify, and some would even applaud.

Stick to the plan. Embrace class and character. Face all adversity with dignity. Have faith, pray for guidance, practice forgiveness and stay focused on your goals.

Let God be the score keeper. He will remember all offenses that go un-confessed and un-absolved. Verses like this one do not just instruct, they predict. All trees are known by their fruit. In the end, all of us will be rewarded according to our deeds.

If your final review came today, how do you think it would go?

DAY 23
You & Work

"Entrust your works to the Lord, and your plans will succeed." Proverbs 16:3

We live and work in a very bottom-line world. Life is hectic. Feeling rushed is common. We frown upon slow developments. We are told to get to the point.

We want fast food, crash diets, express lanes, instant gratification and high-speed everything. We want to be on the ground floor of the next big thing – as long as there is an immediate payoff. We won't take a chance unless there is a guaranteed ROI (return on investment).

With this kind of environment, how would you like a proven strategy for success? Never forget Proverbs 16:3.

Preparing for a meeting? Making a sales call?

Needing to have a difficult conversation? Trying to tackle an overwhelming to-do list? Planning growth? Balancing a budget? Making a command decision? Proverbs 16:3. God enjoys helping us with the details. The events will not always unfold the way we think they should, but with the clarity of hindsight, we will recognize the Lord's involvement in our careers, and become convinced of this Proverb's promise.

Start practicing Proverbs 16:3 today!

DAY 24
You & God

"As for me and my household, we will serve the Lord." Joshua 24:15

Have you declared your allegiance yet? Yes, you may attend Mass on Sunday, but what about your work week? Go ahead and make the commitment, not for others, but for yourself and for your family!

As Catholic professionals, we operate in a cold, grey world of blurred battle fronts where right and wrong are subjective; good and bad are fluid definitions. The quickest way to have the light of truth pierce the clouds, and illuminate your path, is by drawing a line in the sand.

During the presidential election season of 2008, many Americans were panicked by the downturned economy. Pundits and self-proclaimed experts of all types were on cable television, bewildered at the prospect of having to tighten their belts, as they wondered who or what would save them. To me, the answer was obvious.

Once we partner with God, He takes over to calm the storms raging both in and around us, and clears our paths whenever needed. His wisdom is timeless. He is bigger than all our problems combined. There is nothing in our economies or respective industries that He has not foreseen.

His book is the best one on business — and life - ever written. His light will bring refreshing and stabilizing change to your perspective, your profession and your world.

Decide today to reclaim whatever goodness you have stepped away from.

DAY 25
You & God

"His mother said to the servers, 'Do whatever he tells you'." John 2:5

There are many reasons to love Mary. As followers of Christ, we hold her up as a symbol of humility and service. She is the perfect role model for devoutness, quiet strength and steadfastness.

Her story is of a woman not seeking the spotlight, but only the will of God. That openness led her to become the first disciple, while her Lord was still in the womb. It also led her all the way to the foot of the cross, where Jesus put His own suffering aside in His final moments to look after her.

And it is fitting that one of her only direct quotes in Scripture, and her final words in John's Gospel, are meant for us – the modern day servers. Those words are an admonishment and a clarification for us going forward.

Regardless of our current position, as Catholic professionals we all have the same mission – to serve those above us, around us and especially those under us. The higher we climb up the ranks, the greater this responsibility becomes. It is what separates leaders from bosses. The world has enough bosses – and needs more leaders.

DAY 26
You & Others

"If you forgive others their transgressions, your heavenly Father will forgive you. If you do not forgive others, neither will your Father forgive your transgressions." Matthew 6:14-15

How many business decisions are made because people are angry with each other rather than by what makes the most sense? We all tend to invest our time and money according to our feelings. Our human nature has us do the opposite of what we are called to do as Catholic Professionals.

If someone wrongs us, on the job or in traffic, we *think* it is easier to hold grudges, complain, criticize, plot revenge or even update the resume. We blow precious time trying to prove we are right instead of just staying the course and remaining focused on our goals.

Forgiveness is the universal antidote. Resentment only limits you, not the person you resent. Forgiveness frees you. Forgiveness gets your head back in the game faster, because in business, you can't win it, if you're not in it.

I understand that this is easier said than done. I have dealt with professional hurt before. The kind of hurt you bring home with you. It is hard to forgive at times. And even when you first forgive, you will not forget. Here is the reason why:

Forgiveness is a skill that must be developed and practiced. Forgiveness requires a strong — not weak - heart, and the heart must be exercised to handle it. You cannot forgive the big hurts if you cannot first forgive the little ones.

I know this can be as daunting to your spirit and ego as a marathon is to your lungs and legs. So get yourself in the habit. I have found two things that work.

First, every time you recite the Lord's Prayer, and you ask to be forgiven as you forgive those that trespass against you — mean it. Stop and think about everyone that has upset you, since the last time you prayed, and forgive them.

The second is to pray *for* a specific person you need to forgive. This can be a simple petition for God Himself to forgive the person by name, and help you do the same. Or you can take on a larger, concerted effort, like an entire Rosary with the person in mind. This may seem like work, but at times work is required to forgive others and free yourself – especially when you are hurt by a co-worker, key customer or partner. **Do not scoff!** *The reality is you will spend time thinking about the person and/ or incident anyway. Make the time productive for yourself.*

The results are peace and clarity. You will breathe, work and sleep easier when you un-clutter your heart and mind. You will also find more energy to press on towards goals that are bigger than yourself. ***Who do you need to forgive today?***

DAY 27
You & Work

"His master said to him, 'Well done, my good and faithful servant. Since you were faithful in small matters, I will give you great responsibilities. Come, share your master's joy'." Matthew 25:21

Look around your life, your home and business. What we have is from God. It is all His, we are just managing and caretaking portions of His kingdom.

We are here on purpose. We have a job to do, for God. Somehow, for reasons just beyond our reach, we fit into His grand design.

Our unique talents and visions, our positions and present stations, our property, our responsibilities, our money, assets and even our families and people around us all truly belong to Him. Our job is to cultivate, nurture and grow whatever we have. We must bear good fruit. The day will come when we will have a review, and must present our work.

Bigger things are waiting for us if we answer the call, and tend our gardens with care. **What kind of fruit is your garden producing these days?**

DAY 28
You & God

"While they were eating, he took bread, and said the blessing, broke it, and gave it to them, and said, 'Take it; this is my body'." Mark 14:22

The Eucharist is the source, summit and center of the Church's life. As Catholic Professionals, we believe in the True Presence; we believe that consecrated Hosts are the body, blood, soul and divinity of Christ.

This Real Presence is not just available to us at Mass. He is readily available to us throughout the week, in all our tabernacles and Adoration Chapels around the world.

Consider for a moment how many millions of dollars the corporate world spends on consultants, workshops, seminars and motivational speakers each year. Now remember that Jesus Christ is the Highest of High Counsels. He knows everything there is to know about you and your current challenges. And He would love to help you.

Now consider that with Him, there is no gatekeeper. There is no line. There are no fees. You will not be put on hold. There will be no interruptions. You will have His undivided attention.

All we have to do is go visit Him, ask for help and then be quiet. To tap into His wisdom and grace we need to be still. If your parish does not have an Adoration Chapel, just sit near the tabernacle. If the tabernacle doors are closed and there is a candle burning nearby, you can be sure the Blessed Sacrament is secure inside.

Imagine how your relationships and business could benefit from just a 30-60 minute session, once a week, with the guy that has ALL the answers. Go ahead, make the time. And bring your planner with you. He'll help you prioritize everything and find the path to balance.

Enter into His boardroom. The Chairman of chairmen will see you now.

DAY 29
You & Others

"For as in one body we have many parts, and all the parts do not have the same function, so we, though many, are one body in Christ and individually parts of one another." Romans 12:4-5

There is a reason you see things differently from others, interpret what is going on and do things a certain way that is unique to you. God's love for diversity shows up in every group and must be cultivated in our companies.

It is easy to execute a game plan with a hand-picked team. However, life does not always afford us that luxury. It is quite another thing to put together a winning season, year, company or career with the diversity you are dealt.

We all have been made on purpose. We are all

valuable — even those not demonstrating that fact. Our place in time is no accident.

You are in your current position for a reason. You are to make a contribution. The size of the contribution is not determined by us, however the effort is. So dig in. ***Are you meeting today head-on?***

Your place in time is no accident.

DAY 30

You & *Your Business*

Today, you choose.

Open up the Good Book and read whatever you want. Reflect on it as you move about your day. Come tomorrow, repeat.

It is said that if you repeat a behavior for at least three weeks, it becomes a habit. Welcome to the point of this exercise: to get you into the habit of reading the Best Business Book, and the Best Employee Manual, ever written. Use it to grow your relationships, team, sales, company and career.

If you are wondering where to start, I recommend you start the way I did. Pick a Gospel, any of the four. You can't go wrong. I have also taken several examples from Proverbs. **Read it in its entirety to get a master class on handling money, yourself and others.** Then there is always Genesis, the historical roots of God's relationship with man.

Don't forget St. Paul's epistles, letters to the churches he started amongst his travels. St Paul was a divinely inspired traveling salesman. The Psalms are filled with beauty and the books of Daniel and Revelation tickle the imagination.

While you're at it, check out the Catechism's insight and instruction on the Scriptures. It is an invaluable accompaniment. The Bible's applicable wisdom for your life and business is deeper than the oceans, and vaster than space. And it also fits in your purse or briefcase.

Afterword

The power of giving is awesome. **If you found this book useful, please pass it on.** There are Catholic Professionals everywhere. If you will help, we'll get to them all, one reader at a time.

Also, if you have any personal stories about God's Way, helping your own career or business, please share them. They may be included in a future publication. You can reach me through www.Outskirtspress.com/CMB, by just clicking on the "Contact Author" link.

Include all the details in the body of your e-mail. Please, no attachments.

And do not stop there! Help bring *Catholics Mean Business* to your parish and diocese. Send copies to any Catholic business owners, clergy, civic leaders, politicians, military chaplains, journalists, athletes and entertainers you have contact with, or e-mail me the information and I will reach out. Your actions and participation will enable the "100 Year Plan" to succeed!

Relationships Index

Be a part of **Catholics Mean Business'**
<u>100 Year Plan!</u>

Send additional copies to your relatives,
colleagues and clergy!

Please order them at:

<u>WWW.Outskirtspress.com/CMB</u>

<u>WWW.BarnesandNoble.com</u>

<u>WWW.Amazon.com</u>

For details on Speaking Engagements, Parish
Programs,

Fundraising Activities and the "100 Year Plan",
contact

John C. Connell at <u>www.Outskirtspress.com/CMB</u>

LaVergne, TN USA
04 December 2009
165989LV00001B/5/P